# National Security Policy Proceedings

*Volume 1*
*Spring 2010*

FRANK J. GAFFNEY, JR.
*Publisher*

BEN LERNER
*Editor-in-Chief*

DAVID REABOI
*Associate Editor*

© 2010 THE CENTER FOR SECURITY POLICY PRESS
WASHINGTON, DC

securefreedom.org

THE CENTER FOR SECURITY POLICY
1901 Pennsylvania Avenue, Suite 201
Washington, DC 20006
Phone: (202) 835-9077
Email: info@securefreedom.org

For more information, please see **securefreedom.org**

Many of the presentations included in this volume can be found in video form at **youtube.com/securefreedom**

# Contents

# Publisher's Note

## FRANK J. GAFFNEY, JR.

For the past several years, the Center for Security Policy has been privileged to host the biweekly National Security Group Lunch (NSGL) on Capitol Hill. The purpose of the lunch is to foster and inform a community of national security practitioners hailing from the Congress, the executive

Frank J. Gaffney, Jr. is the President and CEO of the Center for Security Policy. Mr. Gaffney formerly acted as the Assistant Secretary of Defense for International Security Policy during the Reagan Administration, following four years of service as the Deputy Assistant Secretary of Defense for Nuclear Forces and Arms Control Policy. Mr. Gaffney is host of Secure Freedom Radio.

branch, the think-tank community, grassroots organizations, academia, the private sector and elsewhere who share a common commitment to the time-tested philosophy Ronald Reagan called "Peace through Strength."

These meetings have a distinguished pedigree. They began decades ago under the sponsorship of the Free Congress Foundation and its founder, Paul Weyrich, an iconic leader of the conservative movement. Mr. Weyrich believed passionately that a commitment to a robust American security posture was, and must be, a touchstone of the movement. To this end, he supported for many years regular meetings of a group he called "the Stanton Coalition."

Starting in early 2007, Paul Weyrich recognized the leadership of the Center for Security Policy for its effective advocacy of sensible, principled foreign and defense policies by inviting the Center to join an organization associated with his Free Congress Foundation, Coalitions for America, in co-hosting these Stanton Coalition meetings. With Mr. Weyrich's much-lamented demise last year, the Center for Security Policy has taken on the sponsorship of these biweekly events, retitled them to reflect their focus and relocated them to the Capitol Visitors Center, the impressive new underground congressional complex adjacent to the Capitol.

It has been my privilege to co-chair these important sessions with one of the most influential members of the senior congressional staff, the Senate Steering Committee's Executive Director, Ed Corrigan. With Ed's leadership, we have striven to make the NSGL's an ever-more-valuable resource to his colleagues on Capitol Hill.

Over the years, the lunches have been addressed by Members of Congress and key members of their staff, former senior executive branch officials, bestselling authors of books with direct relevance to the national security and preemi-

nent scholars with expertise in such topics as: the ideology of jihad, North Korea, Russia, China, nuclear deterrence, the conflicts in Iraq and Afghanistan, border security, Venezuela and other, growing problems in Latin America, the Patriot Act and the International Criminal Court, among many others. Videos of many of these extraordinary presentations are available at the Center for Security Policy's website, **Securefreedom.org**.

In the hope of making the contributions of outstanding security policy practitioners more widely available, the Center is pleased to offer a compilation of our transcripts of such remarks in this new product, National Security Policy Proceedings. In some cases, speakers have chosen to submit their remarks to Proceedings as original articles. Additionally, Proceedings includes book reviews of recently published national security-themed books, reviewed by eminent scholars in the field.

These Proceedings provide the reader with authoritative, yet highly accessible, commentary on the most pressing security policy issues of our time, covering the waterfront of foreign affairs, defense policy, arms control, energy, economic and homeland security. The contents also provide insights into the behind-the-scenes conversations that inform and often shape official decisions. As such, we hope they will become required reading not only for others in the public policy community but for students and responsible citizens, who recognize that an informed electorate is vital to the functioning—and perhaps even the survival—of a republic like ours.

It is a real pleasure to present this inaugural issue of National Security Policy Proceedings and we are gratified at the opportunity it presents to make a significant contribution to the debate on U.S. national security.

Special thanks go to each of our authors for their enormous help with this endeavor, and to my esteemed colleagues at the Center for Security Policy, Director of Policy Operations Ben Lerner and Director of Communications David Reaboi for their service, respectively, as Editor-in-Chief and Associate Editor of the Proceedings. ▪

Frank J. Gaffney, Jr.
President & CEO
Center for Security Policy

# START the Debate

## DOUGLAS J. FEITH

K eeping more nuclear weapons than we need is wasteful, which is why both the United States and Russia have been reducing their arsenals sharply for almost twenty years—since the Cold War ended. Some of the cuts have been taken to fulfill US-Russian treaty

This essay was adapted from remarks by Mr. Feith to the Center for Security Policy's National Security Group Lunch on 18 December, 2009. Mr. Feith, former Under Secretary of Defense for Policy (2001-05), is a Senior Fellow at the Hudson Institute and author of *War and Decision: Inside the Pentagon at the Dawn of the War on Terrorism* (Harper).

obligations—and some were done unilaterally. The Obama administration has just negotiated a new strategic arms reductions treaty with Russia that will require further cuts.

The arms-control argument for reducing nuclear weapons goes beyond the desire to avoid waste. It says that the world necessarily becomes safer and more stable, with less danger of nuclear proliferation, when the numbers of American and Russian nuclear weapons diminish. But that argument doesn't hold water.

Regarding the United States and Russia, the key to peace and stability is the lack of hostility between them—it is not the fine balancing of their respective weapons, or the diminution of their arsenals. And regarding North Korea, Iran and other recent or aspiring nuclear powers, what drives their nuclear programs is unrelated to whether Russia and the United States have twenty or thirty percent fewer warheads or launchers. In fact, at some point, US nuclear weapons cuts might spur proliferation rather than curb it. Many other countries, after all, have foresworn nuclear weapons of their own, relying instead on the American nuclear arsenal to protect them. If the United States were to cut its nuclear capabilities unwisely, American allies and friends might lose confidence in our nuclear assurances and feel compelled to develop their own nuclear weapons. And, potential proliferators might be more inclined to create nuclear arsenals for themselves if their own small arsenals put them close to the capabilities of a greatly diminished US arsenal.

Some US officials have been outspokenly eager, even anxious, for a new strategic arms treaty with Russia. They talk as if the world must under all circumstances improve whenever the United States and Russia agree on additional nuclear weapons reductions.

> *If the United States were to cut its nuclear capabilities unwisely, American allies and friends might lose confidence in our nuclear assurances and feel compelled to develop their own nuclear weapons.*

They claim to be inspired by the hope, championed by President Barack Obama, that the United States can lead the world to eliminate nuclear weapons altogether. There are eminent people who have signed on to this idea. George Shultz and Henry Kissinger, along with other thoughtful people, have endorsed the idea of a nuclear-free world as a US strategic goal.

But nuclear weapons cannot be uninvented. It is not credible that the leadership of every country in the world can be counted on to act in the common interest of humanity by not developing nuclear weapons, especially if developing nuclear weapons could give one a decisive advantage over one's enemies. The notion is so at odds with common sense and with even a basic understanding of history and human nature that its advocacy appears fraudulent. The most charitable view of the nuclear-free world proposal is that its proponents want to tell us something about themselves—about how good and humane they are and about how intensely they would regret the awful consequences of a nuclear war. That's nice to know, of course, but it tells us nothing about the world as it is. It sheds no light on the dangers that good and humane people in the world face from self-aggrandizing brutes and from murderous ideological fanatics. It ignores the unpleasant (some

might say paradoxical) truth that good and humane people sometimes have to use deadly force if they want to maintain their freedom to live good and humane lives.

Some nuclear-free-world advocates admit that circumstances are far from ripe for US nuclear disarmament, and won't be ripe for as far as the eye can see. But they nevertheless champion the idea as a long-term aspiration. They think it has international appeal and will make countries friendlier to the United States. Some think it will discourage nuclear proliferation. But this last point has the same solipsistic flaw as the argument for US-Russian arms control treaties: Countries like North Korea, Iran, Pakistan, India and Israel have their own national security agendas and military concerns and don't organize their lives as responses to American acts of "moral leadership."

Promoting disarmament pie-in-the sky is not cost-free, even as a long-term aspiration. With realistic people, it damages the US government's credibility if our leaders' national security pronouncements sound fantastical. And with people willing to accept the goal of a nuclear-free world at face-value, it distorts their understanding of the security challenges US officials must handle. It undermines popular support for sober US policies.

The Strategic Arms Reduction Treaty (START) signed in

1991 limited the United States and Russia each to 6,000 nuclear warheads. When the Bush administration came into office in 2001, Defense Department officials did a nuclear posture review and decided we didn't need all of the weapons. President Bush then announced in November 2001 that over the next decade we would unilaterally cut our nuclear stockpile down to a range of 1700 and 2200 weapons.

That reduction was based on careful analysis of a complex of concerns. These included warfighting considerations and the assurances the United States has for years provided to allies about the integrity of the US nuclear umbrella. It weighed heavily on us that, if our nuclear commitment to allies came into doubt, some of those allies might develop their own nuclear arsenals. The more countries with nuclear weapons, the greater the chances a nuclear war will occur—and the greater the risk the United States will be harmed either directly or indirectly. For over half a century, the number of nuclear weapons states has remained low and no weapons were detonated in combat. It is a supreme interest of the United States to preserve that restraint—and therefore to maintain a sound US nuclear umbrella.

A month after President Bush announced the planned unilateral US nuclear arms reductions, President Vladimir Putin of Russia declared that his country likewise would unilaterally cut its nuclear arsenal. Russian officials were eager to conclude a new nuclear weapons treaty with us. In general, Bush administration officials were not as eager for a new treaty as were the Russians, for the Cold War was over and we no longer believed that peace with Russia hinged on a nuclear balance of terror. But the Russians clearly wanted to preserve their status as America's nuclear arms control partner. President Bush was willing to conciliate the Russians here, so he agreed to turn his unilateral promise and Putin's into a new agreement that was a formal exchange of promises. This became the Strategic Offensive Reductions Treaty (SORT) that was signed in Moscow in 2002. It obliged the parties to make drastic cuts — approximately 66% — in their strategic offensive weapons. It did no harm because the cuts were sensible in any event, even in the absence of a new treaty. It is not entirely clear that the same can be said for the Obama administration's START follow-on treaty.

The Russians have pushed for the US to destroy weapons rather than disable them and put them in storage. This would provide Russia an asymmetric benefit because Russia maintains a nuclear warhead production capability, while the United States doesn't. For almost two decades the United States has been out of the new war-

*The most charitable view of the nuclear-free world proposal is that its proponents want to tell us something about themselves— about how good and humane they are and about how intensely they would regret the awful consequences of a nuclear war. That's nice to know, of course, but it tells us nothing about the world as it is.*

head production business. If Russia wants to make new nuclear weapons, it can do so almost instantly. The United States, in contrast, would require years to build the production line necessary to create new weapons.

Furthermore, the time it would take for the US to take a set of warheads off the storage shelf and deploy them on missiles would be greater than the time it would take the Russians to produce new weapons. This asymmetry was at the heart of the controversy between the American and Russian negotiators over storing versus destroying weapons.

President Obama has suggested that an arms race would result if there were no START follow-on agreement. Yet post-Cold War history does not support that fear. Both the United States and Russia have unilaterally reduced their arsenals. As noted, nuclear weapons are expensive to maintain. Some weapons age and need to be retired. The START follow-on cannot be justified as the price we have to pay to avert an arms race. We don't have to make concessions to the Russians to pay for reductions they will make anyway for their own reasons.

Is it good or bad for the US and Russia to make another nuclear-arms treaty? There is not necessarily harm in agreeing to some reductions below the levels the Bush administration set with Russia in 2002. The numbers aren't particularly consequential at the margins. An important numbers-related issue is whether the new treaty will allow the United States to maintain the so-called "nuclear triad." As the bipartisan Strategic Posture Commission, led by former Secretaries of Defense William Perry and James Schlesinger, pointed out, preserving a mix of land-based, air-based, and sea-based weapons is valuable for the survivability, flexibility and effectiveness of our nuclear deterrent force.

Other important issues are whether the new treaty will preserve US freedom to add capability to strike targets at long distances with non-nuclear weapons, and whether any of the treaty language will allow Russia to interfere with US plans to build and deploy defenses against missiles of all ranges.

The main argument President Obama has advanced for a new treaty is that it will help us achieve our non-proliferation goals. He is wise to stress the importance of non-proliferation. He evidently does not appreciate, however, how his declarations and policies undermine confidence in US nuclear guarantees and therefore risk bringing about the opposite of his stated intention. His rhetoric about a nuclear-free world, his support for the Comprehensive Test Ban Treaty, his opposition to a new reliable replacement warhead—all cast doubt on the future of the US

policy of "extended deterrence." President Obama is thus calling into question the integrity of the US nuclear umbrella, which (as noted) is a critical element of the international nonproliferation regime.

These issues will be central when the administration presents the new START follow-on treaty to the Senate for approval. Republicans have 41 seats in the Senate, but it only takes 34 votes to block a treaty. And conservative Senators during the Clinton years rejected the CTBT, which boldly announced to the country that the US Senate was no longer an arms-control rubber stamp and was back in the treaty quality-control business. President Obama will have to pay heed to the views of Republicans on this matter.

Led by Senator Jon Kyl, the Senate's Republican caucus has informed President Obama by letter that they will support the new treaty only if it advances US non-proliferation interests, preserves the US nuclear deterrent and the policy of extended deterrence for our friends abroad and protects US rights to build missile defenses – and only if the administration presents a serious plan for modernization of US nuclear weapons infrastructure to make sure that our weapons remain safe and reliable for many years to come.

Now that President Obama has published the new treaty, the debate will begin in earnest. ▪

# Assessing the "Reset" in US-Russia Relations

## DAVID SATTER

My remarks will concern the reset in US-Russian relations. This is a good time to broach the topic because it's been about a year since the term was coined and it's perfectly appropriate that we take a look at what has resulted from a policy which suggested that the fault for the tension in US-Russian relations lay with the US. After all, why should the United States reset its policy if its policy was worthwhile to begin with?

I was recently on an interview program on Arabic al-Jazeera, with a Russian representative, who was able, before an Arab audience, to be considerably less tactful than he would have been if he had been before an audience composed of Westerners. He said that the reset policy was clearly an admission on the part of the United States that the US had hopelessly ruined US-Russian relations. He said that there was no need for concessions on Russia's part. It was up to the US to correct its mistakes.

David Satter is a senior fellow at the Hudson Institute and a fellow of the Foreign Policy Institute of the Johns Hopkins University School of Advanced International Studies (SAIS).

The rationale for this change in policy—announced by Vice-President Biden at the Munich Security Conference—was that we need Russia's help. It is said that none of the major problems in international relations can be solved without the cooperation of Russia. And there are three areas that are frequently mentioned. These are: relations with Iran, nuclear arms reduction talks, and Afghanistan.

In all cases, however, the situation as a result of the reset in relations has not improved and in some respects, it has even gotten worse. In the case of Iran, there are three United Nations resolutions in which sanctions of a sort were mandated for Iran. All of those sanctions were little more than slaps on the wrist as a result of intensive efforts by Russia and China to dilute them.

Has there been a change since then? The answer is no. Instead there has been a rhetorical game in which the president of Russia, Dmitry Medvedev, says that Iran has gone too far, we can't put up with it anymore, and we're ready to consider sanctions. And then Sergey Lavrov, the Russian foreign minister replies that actually Iran is being perfectly cooperative and there is no reason why any change should be inaugurated. And as a result, the situation remains what it was, Russians continue to provide black market aid and advice to Iran as well as diplomatic coverage and

*In all cases, however, the situation as a result of the reset in relations has not improved and in some respects, it has even gotten worse.*

Iran continues in its efforts to make nuclear weapons and the threat to the world that Iran represents increases.

The situation is similar with the nuclear arms reduction talks. The last START treaty expired in December. There was a hope expressed by the Obama administration that it would be possible to have a new treaty in place before the expiration of the old one. This did not happen. But the greater question, and the more pivotal one from the point of view of the national security of the United States, is whether we need such a treaty at all. Russian nuclear experts and independent defense analysts have affirmed that Russia will not as a result of the envisaged treaties be retiring a single workable nuclear weapon. They will be retiring those weapons whose service life has expired.

The United States, however, will be forced to make real cuts. It's not inconceivable that even such a seemingly one-sided agreement could be in the interests of the United States. But what is disquieting are the justifications that are used for this agreement.

One justification is that we're paving the way for a world without nuclear weapons, which is unrealistic under circumstances in which Iran and North Korea are frantically trying to develop them and Russia not only has no plans to eliminate nuclear weapons, but

makes nuclear weapons the linchpin of its security policy and is lowering the threshold for their use.

The other justification is that this will establish that we respect Russia, that we recognize Russia as a great power. But why should we do such a thing? Is it really important for US security that we encourage Russia to think that it's something that it's not? And what are the likely consequences of this misperception on the part of Russia?

We've seen that Russia has a proclivity for attacking its neighbors and putting pressure on them. We need only to refer to the war in Georgia in August, 2008. Russia is building new military bases in Abkhazia, an area that it separated from Georgia, a sovereign nation, while waging a genocidal war to prevent separation on the part of Chechnya from Russia.

So in the matter of strategic arms reduction talks it's hard to see that the reset has brought any meaningful benefit to the United States. President Medvedev did announce and in this respect, his announcement has been backed up by action, that goods, including lethal cargos, intended for Afghanistan, can now transit Russia.

But here again, there's a paradox. We have to ask ourselves, why Russia should have ever refused cooperation with our efforts to remove a grave threat to the world, but in particular to Russian national security, posed by Islamic extremists in Afghanistan? Is this not a case of creating a problem in order to resolve it and then take credit for the resolution?

In addition to these strategic issues, an unannounced, but nonetheless important consequence of the reset has been silence on the part of the United States regarding human rights violations in Russia. The dismantling of democracy and killing of human rights activists and journalists who dare to publish truthful articles is continuing in Russia. There is no mass terror in Russia. There is not even mass repression. There's a level of freedom that, to be fair, is far greater than anything that existed under the Soviet Union. But there is selective terror and those people who seek to resist the authoritarian practices of the regime are eliminated one by one.

This tendency cripples the ability of Russian society—which is battered under any circumstances by the impact of years of economic turmoil—to assert its rights against a regime which is seeking to become permanent with a president for life.

I know some will object that there's a new president. Dmitry Medvedev. But in fact the new president is controlled by the old president, so we can really speak of Russia being ruled by a president for life.

In sum, the scorecard for the change in policy that was supposed to create a new, more cooperative Russia, is extremely discouraging. The United States has gained little from admitting to mistakes that it never made. And the long-term effect may well be not to charm the Russians, but to embolden them to act in ways that are contrary to American interests.

Russian objections to American activities in the Ukraine were not based on any real fear of interference by the US but rather on fear that Ukraine would be in a position to assert its independence vis-à-vis Russia. The most recent Ukrainian election shows that there is a workable democratic system in Ukraine. Operating from our assumptions, we might say to the Russians "Your guy was defeated in the Orange Revolution. But, nonetheless, now he's back in power. And this is the nature of democracy that while you lose power, you can still fight to get it back."

But the Russian leaders do not care whether democracy works or does not work. They're concerned that Ukraine is not completely controllable by them. And as long as the United States stands behind a process which will make that difficult, that will be a source of tension. And if there are no obvious ways in which to stir up that tension, they'll invent some.

*The United States has gained little from admitting to mistakes that it never made. And the long-term effect may well be not to charm the Russians, but to embolden them to act in ways that are contrary to American interests.*

Iran is a country with a very young population. Russia has an aging population. And the day will come when the demographic balance between those two countries will be considerably less favorable to Russia than it is now. And that day will be soon. Russia has every reason to be concerned about a nuclear weapon in the hands of the fanatical and bloodthirsty Iranian clerics.

But they also understand that, by backing Iran, they make themselves important in world affairs. If Russia were cooperating with the West, there would be no reason for the Western countries to be spending huge amounts of mental energy trying to come up with ways to influence Russia to do what it should have been doing in the first place. And by making itself a problem, it creates a situation in which Russia's profile and influence in world affairs, albeit in a negative sense, is greatly increased. And this is something that they do not want to give up.

The national interests of Russia are not identical to the selfish interests of the small group of people who run the country. And it is the ambitions of this small group which make Russia a poor candidate for integration with the West, which inevitably requires respect for human rights, the rule of law, and decent behavior, as well as democracy. You can't have a president for life in a country that's an integral part of the Western alliance.

To preserve Russia's oligarchic structure of power and the corrupt and aggressive regime that is based on it it is necessary for Russia to seek not points of contact with the West, but points of conflict. And that's what the Russian leaders do.

There's a tradition in Russia of lack of respect for the individual that goes back hundreds of years. It is only by establishing once and for all that the individual human being has some inherent worth, and making that the cornerstone of the social structure that the problem of values in Russia can really be solved.∎

# 9/11: Eight Years Later

## WALID PHARES

In the next several minutes I will present a retrospective summary and analysis of events that have transpired since 9/11 and identify the Jihadist forces responsible for those events. I do not pretend in my presentation today to have a solution for every challenge America is facing in its ongoing confrontation with Jihadist forces at home and abroad. Nor will I address the myriad details of secondary importance in order that I may leave with you today, an unobstructed strategic view of the conflict and its evolution since September 11, 2001.

Eight years after that fateful day, Washington, DC and America's citizens remain divided between two perspectives regarding the exact nature of the conflict and what to do about it. The always imminent Jihadist threat to our way of life is in addition to the risks that continue to accrue to ours and other Western societies as

Dr. Walid Phares is a Senior Fellow with the Foundation for the Defense of Democracies and the author of *The Confrontation: Winning the War against Future Jihad*. Dr. Phares teaches Global Strategies at the National Defense University in Washington and advises the Anti-Terrorism Caucus at the US House of Representatives. His web site is **walidphares.com**.

we continue to equivocate over the exact nature of the threat. This reluctance to acknowledge the obvious has left the West's underbelly exposed and hampered efforts to develop sound mitigation strategies.

Allied objectives in World Wars I and II were crystal clear from the time the first shots were fired. Allied forces knew exactly who the enemy was and the objectives they must meet to end the conflict. By the time five years had passed after America entered World War II, Allied forces had reduced German, Italian, and Japanese fascist regimes to rubble, celebrating Victory in Europe Day (V-E Day) on May 12, 1945 and Victory in the Pacific Day (V-P or V-J Day) only three months later on August 15 of that same year. Only three years after the end of World War II and eight years after its start, the West found itself embroiled in the Cold War with the Soviet Union and Marxist ideology.

Today we are eight years into the confrontation with Jihadists and we still do not know who our enemy is, the objectives we need to pursue, or the best strategy for accomplishing those objectives.

Anyone who understands "war of ideas" knows that failure to identify and characterize the Jihadist threat is a recipe for sure defeat. While senior bureaucrats in Washington continue to act as if

*The post-9/11 debate over the Jihadists identity and ideology has been confused and yielded little fruit. Eight years after 9/11 we remain conflicted over the topology of the Jihadist forces arrayed against us and the reasons for their hostility toward us.*

Jihad is yoga, our enemies continue to execute their strategy to take down the West. Jihad as yoga may make sense if one is attempting to illustrate absurdity with the absurd, but in the real world, minimizing the Jihadist threat will only serve to weaken our resolve at a time we can least afford it. How can we succeed against an enemy we refuse to acknowledge? As an historian, I can imagine future historians' incredulity when they look back and discover that eight years into this conflict, America remained dubious about the identity of its enemy.

For a moment, let's consider the 9/11 Jihadist's identity as an academic topic, concerning which there are two schools of thought. The first view accurately portrays the attacks of 9/11 as an al-Qaeda operation. However, this view often includes the notion that al-Qaeda only represents a small group of fringe radicals out of the global, predominantly "moderate" Muslim population. This school of thought also argues that the US was attacked because of its foreign policy. The second school of thought attributes the attacks of 9/11 to al-Qaeda, and views al-Qaeda as another stage in the evolution of Jihadist history, a single variant among the vast nebula of Jihadist forces spanning the globe. This is the correct school and the one with which I identify. This view also argues that

individual Jihadists belong to one of two ideological families. The first is populated with Salafists whose emergence we are now witnessing around the globe. The al-Qaeda terrorists who attacked us on 9/11 were Salafists. The second is populated with Jihadi Khomeinists and includes the terrorists who bombed the US Marine barracks in Lebanon in 1983, killing 941 US Marines. The Jihadi Khomeinists' mobilization against the United States has continued unabated since that time.

The post-9/11 debate over the Jihadists identity and ideology has been confused and yielded little fruit. Eight years after 9/11 we remain conflicted over the topology of the Jihadist forces arrayed against us and the reasons for their hostility toward us. Many of us are still asking, *"Why do they hate us?"* Are the Jihadists a vast network or a fringe group? Are we being relentlessly attacked because of our foreign policy, or the Jihadists' ideology? The absence of a battle strategy is evidenced by opposing responses to the Jihadist forces arrayed against us. Our forces are in disarray while Jihadi forces continue their steady march forward.

In 2001, with the full support of the American people and Congress, US military forces deployed to Afghanistan to fight the "big network" of Jihadists. Thus we crumbled the Taliban regime in a war of necessity, as it is characterized today. US-led coalition forces then entered Iraq to remove Saddam Hussein, in a military campaign that was hotly contested both in the US and abroad. I agree with many observers who posit that the Iraq campaign wasn't as much about necessity as it was a strategy to deal with the wider confrontation. The reasons and motives for the Iraq campaign should have been articulated more clearly to the American electorate and our allies abroad.

Of the Jihadist forces that joined the battle with US troops in Iraq and Afghanistan between 2001 and 2006, not all were al-Qaeda from the Sunni Triangle. Jihadists from other regions joined the fight as well, including the entire Taliban network in Afghanistan and Pakistan. Jihadists in other theaters also began to engage allied troops and the conflict widened as it did during World War I, which began in Sarajevo and spread across the entire European continent; World War II unfolded in similar fashion. The continuing conflict with Jihadists exhibits many of the characteristics of a conventional confrontation that uses unconventional means similar to those of Somalia's Shabab Mujahideen, except that the Mujahideen Jihadists have been joined by al Qaeda affiliates from the Sahel of Africa, Pakistan, Indonesia, and the Philippines. Other countries such as Russia, Great Britain and Spain which criticized or did not participate in the US campaigns were still attacked later by the same Jihadi network.

How can we best characterize the last eight years of the "War on Terror" which I describe in my books as a *"relentless Jihadi war on democracies?"* Today in the West we have a choice between engagement and disengagement; the Jihadists have no plans to disengage. They can cease firing, move plans from the front to the back burner or the other way around. One stream can engage us with weapons while another, such as the Iranian regime, builds a thermonuclear weapon. One stream can retreat while another attacks us. Military strategists understand that global conflicts unfold in this way.

We spent seven of the last eight years in this "War on Terror" engaging the Jihadists. This last and eighth year we have been in retreat on every front. I am not trying to sensationalize the risk, nor do I speak from a political perspective. I speak to you today as an academic whose analysis indicates *intentional* disengagement. While it is possible that the citizens of this country would still disengage after being armed with the information I am giving you today, they must at a minimum

*Denial is the quickest and surest pathway to defeat. If this confrontation is not about Jihadist ideology, then there is no "war of ideas." If there is no ideology to foment Jihad, then there is no Jihad. To suggest otherwise in the face of a vast and growing body of evidence to the contrary, amounts to sociopolitical suicide.*

understand that we have entered the era of disengagement.

The first seven years of this conflict can be partitioned further. From 2001 to 2003, the United States was on the offensive, toppling the Taliban regime first, and then Saddam's regime. Since then we have spent five years in a stalemate with Jihadi forces in what could be described as trench warfare. The US has never adopted a cohesive strategy in the War on Terror, perhaps because defeating the Taliban in Afghanistan came relatively easily. The bigger challenge facing us after defeating the Taliban is the battle for the hearts and minds of the citizenry.

Denial is the quickest and surest pathway to defeat. If this confrontation is not about Jihadist ideology, then there is no "war of ideas." If there is no ideology to foment Jihad, then there is no Jihad. To suggest otherwise in the face of a vast and growing body of evidence to the contrary, amounts to sociopolitical suicide. If we will but acknowledge the ideology that continually spawns new Jihadists and the Jihad, we will already be halfway down the road to victory. We *must* begin to focus our attention and efforts on the ideology. We must learn everything there is to know about the ideology so we can field effective ideological countermeasures.

This war will not be won with strategic communications blitzes and slick public relations campaigns, beneficial though they might be. We and our trusted allies in other civil societies must stand firmly in solidarity with one another as we seek to confront Jihadist ideology in our cities, towns and local communities. The United States had the necessary financial and logistical resources to fight an ideological war, but it lacked the political and strategic will. The prior Administration delivered compelling speeches during its tenure, but subordinate levels of Government did not follow through with an execution strategy. In some agencies, not one of the Bush Administration's policies was implemented.

The United States is facing an ideology that is a much bigger threat than the forces we have been confronting in Afghanistan, Iraq and elsewhere. In the War of Ideas, we are confronting immense and powerful lobbies and financial interests that are nourished by revenues from oil exporting regimes. Let me be very clear; there are hardcore elements in OPEC that are aligned with hardcore elements in the Organisation of the Islamic Conference (OIC). Though the OIC is not fighting on the battlefields of Iraq and Afghanistan, they provide a second strategic line of defense in the form of Jihadist ideology. Whenever someone begins to emphasize the role of ideology in

the confrontation, these organizations mobilize their forces to discredit every fact about the Jihad. They do not try to prevent us from fighting al-Qaeda because al-Qaeda is not the actual factory that produces al-Qaeda and the Jihadists. The real factory is Jihadism, but the Jihadists insist that their ideology is off limits.

Those of us fighting the War of Ideas have gone back and forth trying to figure out what is going on. We are in a war with the terrorists, but every time we come close to identifying the Jihadi Salafists or Jihadi Khomeinists as an ideological threat to our national security, there is a blockade in Washington, DC and Brussels. I understand this to be the phenomenon that transformed the war from an offensive struggle during the first two years, to a stalemate fought in the trenches.

What kept the United States from completing the task of flushing the Jihadists who had penetrated our defenses? What kept us from supporting other friends of democracy and the primary victims of Jihad, women and minorities? We were not permitted to identify the ideological nature of the battle because as it is the ideology of al-Qaeda, Hezbollah, Jamaa Islamiyah, and the Taliban, it is also the ideology of the oil-producing regimes that have been funding its propagation for decades. If we try to project democracy in the region, we threaten those interests as well.

In summary, two years on the offensive, five years in a stalemate, and a general retreat in 2009 says we are disengaging from Iraq without containing Iran. We are not "meddling" in support of democracy in Iran (I use "meddling" intentionally here). We are talking to Bashar al-Assad. We may be talking to Hezbollah. In the Afghan theater where our troops are fighting the Jihadists, we are searching for "good" Taliban that we may engage them. This is a long war and it will be much longer unless the American public comes to realize, before it is too late, that the Jihadists are always at war with us even after we disengage. ∎

# Define the Enemy: What It Takes to Win in Afghanistan

## ALLEN B. WEST

I spent twenty-two years, active duty service, in the United States Army, and spent two-and-a-half years, from June of 2005 to November of 2007, in Kandahar, Afghanistan. During that time, I was a civilian-military senior advisor to the Afghanistan National Army in conjunction with the United States Army and also NATO forces, responsible for the southern region.

But before I begin, there are three basic quotes that I want to share with you that I think apply to what's going on in Afghanistan. The first one comes from the Chinese military philosopher Sun-Tzu, who said "to know your enemy and to know yourself and to know the terrain or the environment in countless amounts of battles, you will always be victorious."

The second quote came to me from a retired Marine First Sergeant by the name of Jim Reifinger

Lieutenant Colonel Allen West (U.S. Army, Retired) was battalion commander for the Army's 4th Infantry Division during Operation Iraqi Freedom, and previously served as a senior advisor to the Combined Security Transition Command in Afghanistan.

who explained to me, " if you ever find yourself in a fair fight, it is because your tactics suck."

The last quote is something to which we all need to pay attention. And this was something that I taught my soldiers when I was in Iraq, mentored Afghan officers on, and continue to share whenever I can. It is the simple maxim that, *the reality of your enemy must, or eventually will, become your own.*

When I am asked, "Col. West, are we winning in Afghanistan?" I give a simple response. If we were winning in Afghanistan we would not be conducting major combat operations some nine years after we engaged the Taliban in that Theater of Operations.

One of the major problems that we have when analyzing Afghanistan is our persistent denial of the enemy against whom we are fighting and how to confront him. I want to address the tactical level up to the operational and strategic level, how we need to have a meshing of tasks to make sure that we are properly prosecuting this thing called a War on Terror, which for me is a terrible misnomer.

You may recall that General Richard E. Cavazos commanded every level, from the Platoon all the way up to US Army Forces Command, retiring as a four-star general. Any time he evaluated a combat commander as part of the Army Senior leader mentoring program, Cavazos would ask a very simple

*At the tactical level of the fight we have five basic tasks that we have to accomplish: find the enemy, fix him in position, engage him with your weapons systems, defeat him, and then you must pursue him. The United States military forces will never lose at the tactical level, because our Soldiers, Sailors, Marines, and Airmen are the best in the world, when empowered to conduct well-conceived tactical operations.*

question: Is your operation enemy-oriented or is your operation terrain-oriented? The answer to this question helps the Combat Commander focus operations on the tasks to be accomplished.

At the tactical level of the fight we have five basic tasks that we have to accomplish: *find* the enemy, *fix* him in position, *engage* him with your weapons systems, *defeat* him, and then you must *pursue* him. The United States military forces will never lose at the tactical level, because our Soldiers, Sailors, Marines, and Airmen are the best in the world, when empowered to conduct well conceived tactical operations.

However, where we always seem to find a problem is when we transition from the tactical to the middle or operational level, and eventually the strategic level.

We saw an example of this at the end of 2009 when our President had issues with the timely development of his strategic goals and objectives for the Operational theater commander General Stanley McChrystal.

We have been at this operation in Afghanistan for almost nine years. When have we ever heard a Commander-in-Chief definitively outline the strategic level goals and objectives in prosecuting this thing called the Global War on Terror? Certainly President Obama's plan issued at the US Military Academy, West Point did not suffice. It was just another speech. Indeed, Afghanistan and our national security was not even a focused topic of the 2010 State of the Union address.

What are the strategic objectives? The first thing we fail to understand is that Afghanistan is not a war in and of itself. Neither was Iraq a war in and of itself. These are both theaters of operation in a wider global conflagration. This first true battle is indicative of what the 21st century battlefield will entail—it is political, it is informational, it is military, and it is also economic. We are not using all of our elements of national power to prosecute the enemy at the strategic level.

At the strategic level, there are several things we should be looking at, assuming we are properly focused on being enemy-oriented, and not terrain-oriented. When you are terrain-oriented, you become an Army of occupation, more concerned about holding land than focusing on the enemy—I'll tie that up at the end.

What we need to look at doing, first and foremost, is denying this enemy a sanctuary *wherever* he seeks to establish himself. We have not done a good job of doing this, but we are improving. We also need to interdict his flow of men, materiel, and financial support. A key strategic and operational task is to separate the radical Islamic foe from his major funding sources: oil revenues and opium. Third, we need to understand how we cordon off the areas of operation in which we are operating. You almost have to put a bubble around these areas to keep the enemy infiltration out. The last thing that we have to do from a strategic and operational standpoint is win the information operation. We have to influence the greater population against this enemy -- that includes here on the home front. And we have to understand that the true power in places like Iraq and Afghanistan and in the Islamic world lies not with leaders such as Mahmoud Ahmadinejad or with Hamid Karzai, but rather with the mullahs, the clerics, and the imams.

I had a great discussion when I was over in Afghanistan with a state department official. I asked, why don't we, on these Afghan military bases that we're building, put radio stations there? This would enable our Coalition forces to start broadcasting messages out, since in Afghanistan, you have about a 70% overall illiteracy rate. But they love music and they listen to the radio. How better to combat against the Taliban and what they're doing than to get your message out there? And get it out there with Afghan soldiers that are serving their country developing a sense of pride and a national character.

The official looked at me and stated that it would probably be too hard and we probably would not be able to broadcast all over the country. I had offered a simple solution that was disregarded— one that would have helped us win.

The heroin trade is the number one means by which the Taliban is getting its financial support. Some people are talking about how we are doing poppy eradication over in Afghanistan. What was occurring was elimination of the competition, since certain poppy fields did not get touched in Afghanistan. Everyone in southern Afghanistan knew that Hamid Karzai's brother was one of the prominent war lords and drug dealers.

If you're a farmer, here in the United States of America, and you're just trying to earn a living, and someone comes in and plows up your field, and takes away your livelihood, is that person endeared to you or do you start to see that person as an enemy? The Taliban has taken poppy eradication and turned it against us by going in and providing security to these farmers, taking the poppy, and then going out and selling it. These farmers don't care who they sell it to. They just want to live. We should be providing some type of security to them going in; we can buy this crop up. We can burn it or we can seek to convert it into morphine or something positive while also transitioning these farmers to another crop for a livelihood. We cannot allow this crop to continue to fall into the hands of the Taliban,

*We can execute the synergistic employment of these weapons systems, but the [Rules of Engagement] must support their utilization. Allowing the enemy to preclude their usage because of their demonic use of civilian shields has to be stopped.*

which of course they in turn use for men, materiel, and financial support.

One of the most critical aspects of combat operations we must analyze, and correct, from the strategic level down to the tactical level is the Rules of Engagement (ROE). The current rules of engagement have been so terribly drawn up that they now provide the enemy the advantage. We are allowing the enemy to pin down our forces before we engage with all available weapons systems. The Taliban knows what we will and will not do, and they exploit that to their advantage, often to the detriment of our men and women on the ground. We do not need to create a "fair fight" environment. It is imperative that we use every advantage our highly trained and technologically advanced military has at its disposal, to include owning the night and conducting operations during limited visibility.

The enemy in Afghanistan, and elsewhere, knows that our ROE are based on the enemy conveying hostile intent, defined as their having weapons and firing. The strategic and operational level decision-making processes that created these rules are preventing our soldiers from properly engaging this enemy and defeating him.

Back in 2006, [then-President of Pakistan, Gen.] Pervez Musharraf, along with Lieutenant General Richards, who was the commander of the NATO forces in Afghanistan at that time, drew up an agreement whereby the Pakistani army pulled out of the Northwest Frontier Tribal Provinces area, which we refer to as Waziristan. As soon as that withdrawal took place, we saw everything come into that harsh, remote mountainous area. And, of course, the attacks spiked monumentally in eastern and southern Afghanistan. We have to stop creating a sanctuary for this enemy. We have to reach out and strike this enemy wherever he presents himself. Do we need more troops going into Afghanistan? Yes, we do in order to dry up the sanctuary of operations the enemy utilizes. However, that is not the only and exact answer to problem in Afghanistan.

We can use more unmanned aerial vehicles (UAVs) or "drones" as they have come to be known. We can use attack helicopters, which are a very powerful tool in that mountainous type of terrain as well as fixed-wing attack aircraft, an A-10 type platform would be ideal. Another superb aerial weapons delivery platform is the AC-130 Spectre gunship, as used by our Air Force Special Operations Forces. We have to be able to track this enemy and bring those systems to bear. One of the great systems we have is a surface-to-surface system called the multiple-launch rocket system (MLRS), especially the wheeled version called HIMARS.

We can execute the synergistic employment of these weapons systems, but the ROE must support their utilization. Allowing the enemy to preclude their usage because of their demonic use of civilian shields has to be stopped.

Our defense industry must be a partner on the battlefield of the 21st century by developing weapon systems that align with the nature of the threat, and its defeat. We can ill afford to have a defense industry that produces materiel based upon what they desire to sell. We should be paying more attention to what the young Officers and Non-Commissioned Officers recommend to fight this adaptive and agile enemy.

Another thing that hurts us in Afghanistan is the respective NATO member troop employment criteria and directives called the NATO Caveats, which detail what the member nations will and will not do. If we had fought World War II the same way that we are fighting in Afghanistan, a whole lot of people would have been speaking German or Japanese.

Provinces and areas are assigned to respective Countries, and a good number of these Countries first answer to their Ministry of Defense, not the Operational Commander on the ground. This not only causes consternation for the Commander, it also allows the enemy to assess where he can have sanctuary, the "path of least resistance." Furthermore, it creates an "us vs. them" mentality within coalition forces on the ground, as some nations pull a much heavier weight than others. Lastly, this can result in a coordination nightmare for communications and cross-zone combat operations.

It is not always about more troops; it is about proper resourcing and truly operating in a combined theater of operations, with unity of command and unity of effort.

So what do I say we need to do? First: We should have been focused on security and the enemy before we got involved in the political or nation-building aspect. It is called the Islamic Republic of Afghanistan. In Islam, there is no regard for secular government. All laws, everything that governs the people, come from the Koran. If you seek to establish democracy in an Islamic republic, you are promoting ideals that contradict the most fundamental principle of Islam. This goes back to what Sun-Tzu said: know the environment or terrain. This is something that we must understand at the strategic and the operational level.

Schools being opened are a great thing. But at night, or in broad daylight, the Taliban comes in and destroys those schools. If we cannot provide security, young girls will still have acid thrown on them or be gunned down when they walk away from those schools.

We must get off the expansive terrain-oriented bases we have established in Afghanistan and get our troops out in the field to deny the enemy freedom of maneuver, day or night.

In closing, the War on Terror is a worldwide conflagration—it is not a fight against a tactic, terror, but rather against a totalitarian theocratic-political ideology. It is not restricted to any certain country or any certain theater of operation. And if we do not start developing the goals and objectives at the strategic level, bringing it down to the operational level, and nesting it to what our men and women are doing on the ground, we're going to walk the same path that we walked in Vietnam.

We cannot afford to lose to this enemy. This is a fight that has been going on since 622 AD—we are just a new chapter in an ages-long struggle. This enemy will not concede, and we must never give up. We cannot allow this to continue for another nine years due to our inability to clearly identify the enemy and soundly defeat him. ▪

# Preventing Terrorist Travel

## PAUL ROSENZWEIG

My theme is the Christmas day plot and Umar Farouk Abdulmutallab's attempt to bomb the Northwest flight landing in Detroit. To give you the bottom line up front, my thesis is simple: we did it to ourselves. Which is to say that the near

Mr. Rosenzweig is Principal, Red Branch Consulting, PLLC and Visiting Fellow at the Heritage Foundation's Davis Institute for International Studies. Mr. Rosenzweig served as the Deputy Assistant Secretary for Policy at the Department of Homeland Security from 2005 to 2009. This paper reflects the substance of a presentation made to a Center for Security Policy meeting on February 26, 2010.

success of plots like this is an inevitable result of policy and legal decisions that have been made in this Congress and by this Administration and, candidly, by the prior Administration to forgo the ability to conduct the sorts of information analysis that would have potentially revealed the plot.

What do I mean by that? The Christmas plot was not a failure of intelligence collection. There was quite a bit of intelligence about Abdulmutallab. According to the New York Times, there was an NSA intercept about a Nigerian training in Yemen with Christmas plans.

There was our understanding from the Saudis of plans by al-Qaeda to place bombs in underwear, or other clothing. There was the report from his father that Abdulmutallab had been radicalized and gone to Yemen. There was a partial name in one intercepted al-Qaeda communication regarding someone named Umar Farouk. There was the fact that the UK had denied this fellow a visa. And of course there was the fact that we, ourselves, had given him one. That's quite a bit of information.

The problem is that it's ten bits of information, more or less, floating in a sea of millions. The National Counterterrorism Center (NCTC) has links to eighty separate data bases. They're the people, along with the CIA, who are responsible today for connecting the dots in the way that the 9/11 Commission called for. In these eighty different databases, they get tens of thousands of pieces of new intelligence every day. They get over a thousand new names to think about and consider for inclusion in terrorist information databases every day. They add three hundred and fifty new names to the Terrorist Information Datamart Environment (TIDE)—our basic watch list of terrorists—every single day.

Now, hindsight is 20/20. Lifting those ten different bits of information out of that sea and flood, we can readily say that it would have been better had somebody

*What the Christmas plot was a failure of, was not a failure of intuition, but rather a failure of time and capacity. The NCTC still lacks the technical tools that are necessary to enable analysts to conduct the sort of analysis that would actually produce the results we're seeking to achieve.*

recognized that we need to look for Nigerians connected to Yemen. Or that we needed to look for somebody whose name or part of whose name is Umar Farouk. And it is certainly the case that it would have been much better had the ideas of "Yemen" and "Nigerian plot" somehow moved to the top of analysts' piles.

But the truth of the matter is that when that question moves up, something else has to move down. So what the Christmas plot was a failure of, was not a failure of intuition, but rather a failure of time and capacity. The NCTC still lacks the technical tools that are necessary to enable analysts to conduct the sort of analysis that would actually produce the results we're seeking to achieve.

What do I mean by that? Let's take one example. The NCTC does not still today have an ability to "google" a particular name across all eighty of its databases—in other words they can't conduct a simple natural language search of the sort that thousands of Americans do every minute on Google or Yahoo. Why not? To a large degree, it's because the eighty databases are all in disparate forms, and they are not commensurate with each other. So today you cannot, if you are an analyst, when you get an intelligence lead about someone named "Umar Farouk," type in, in a single place, a query: "what do we know about Umar Farouk?" and

get a Google-type list of pages that have other intelligence information about the name Umar Farouk. It's just not technologically feasible. Instead each separate database must be individually queried—a time consuming process.

But worse yet, even if we had that "Google" capacity, the results wouldn't be enough to really enable our analysts to do what they want to do. If you typed in Umar Farouk, or if you picked perhaps a slightly more common name, like Umar Mohammed, you would literally get thousands, if not tens of thousands, if not hundreds of thousands, of pages with information—different little bits of intelligence information about Umar Farouk or Umar Mohammed or whatever the name is that you're interested in. Nobody could possibly review them all. An so what we really need, and what we lack, are better automated analytical tools that will allow that kind of analysis to go on in the background at the level of an automated artificial intelligence system.

For example, we don't currently use a system that incorporates the concept of "persistent queries." Here's how that concept works: You ask a question, "Do we know anything about Umar Farouk?" And the answer comes back: "No we don't know anything." Okay. That's great. That's the end of it today.

What we need to develop are systems where that query, that question, resides permanently as a question in the database so that it is itself a piece of intelligence. So, for example, when the NSA gets an intercept with the name Umar Farouk, and asks "do we know anything about Umar Farouk," that resides permanently in the databases. And even if the answer is "nothing right now," when six weeks later, a State Department intelligence report comes in and says, "somebody named Abdulmutallab has come into the Nigerian embassy and provided us with information about his son Umar Farouk Abdulmutallab, who he thinks has gone to Yemen and been radicalized," those two pieces of information, the query, from six weeks ago (or two years ago), and the new intelligence information from today, link up together.

That's what we call, in analysis systems, the concept of persistence in data queries. We don't do that right now. We also don't tag data so that information can be corrected. One of the things that it has been suggested happened in this case was that initially the name was misunderstood or mistyped so that it wasn't "Umar Farouk," but a different name. And then the correction came out later and it never caught up with the original erroneous data. That's because when we send new data out into the intelligence space, we don't tag it so that

later corrections by intelligence analysts that revise the data catch up with the original piece of information that moves forward.

All of this is designed to prevent what we call enterprise amnesia. Enterprise amnesia is when the enterprise, the intelligence collection and analysis enterprise, has so much information that it forgets what it knows. And can't remember, from day to day, that the NSA was interested in Umar Farouk, that the NSA had an intercept about a Nigerian and that now, we've got a Nigerian father with a son named Umar Farouk who has come into our embassy. So why is this so? Because our analysts don't have time to do this sort of cataloging.

Our computers do. But we haven't developed the tools to let them do it. Why not? Because we decided we didn't want them.

We started to develop these tools back in the immediate aftermath of 9/11, but Congress killed a large fraction of the program. It was called Total Information Awareness, which was a pretty scary and not very user-friendly name, but the idea that was being developed in DARPA (the Defense Advanced Research Projects Agency) was to develop a whole suite of these tools like persistent data queries.

They were also developing visualization tools to allow analysts to see the data. Instead of just hav-

*We've come to the conclusion that arming the police has a greater benefit for us—that is, the prevention of general crime within society—than we fear the costs of the occasional instances of misuse. The same ought to be true in the intelligence analytical space.*

ing lots of little pages that come back in a Google search page, visualization tools allow them to see pictures of connections of the data.

By and large, because of privacy concerns, we killed a large fraction of the research under that program. It has been reported that some of the research continues in a classified space but the public research, the work that that the Department of Defense was doing, is dead and has not been funded since 2003.

What we need most of all is to actually change how we think about these analytical tools and change how we think about the privacy implications of their use. What killed this set of programs in the first instance was fears of Big Brother. There was a wonderful, horrible article by William Safire, called "You Are A Suspect" in which he posited that allowing artificial analytical tools like these to operate would allow the US government to collect and create a dossier on every individual in America. And eventually to run the same intelligence analytics that track terrorists in a way that would track political opponents, instead. Or to track deadbeat dads or some other less serious offense.

I suppose, in theory, that's right. The tools themselves are neutral as to the subject matter to which you put them. But the right answer is not prohibition, as we've now done for the past 5 years. The right answer, of course, is regulation, oversight, training, and effective response when there are errors. Use a strong audit capacity, if you want, to find those who abuse the system.

To take a very prosaic example, we do not say that because some policemen accidentally shoot the wrong person or because some policemen even go further and misuse their weapons and shoot a friend with whom they have an argument, that we should forgo giving guns to police officers. Instead we say that we want to train them, we want to pick them carefully, we want to have internal affairs bureaus when they misuse their weapons, and, if need be, we want to fire them and criminally prosecute them for the abuse.

Why do we do that? Because we've come to the conclusion that arming the police has a greater benefit for us—that is, the prevention of general crime within society—than we fear the costs of the occasional instances of misuse. The same ought to be true in the intelligence analytical space. We can acknowledge that there is a possibility of misuse and abuse down the road. Anybody who knows some of the history of the intelligence community can't say that it never happens. But instead of saying, this is a technique and a technology we will no longer use, we should say that we need to conduct oversight and audits of the

programs that are put into place and when there are abuses, punish them severely.

We're actually moving in that direction a little bit recently. One story to think about is the incident in the last presidential campaign where it was said that some people had looked at then-candidate Obama's passport files in the State Department. Most everybody remembers that. And that would be this sort of abuse. The inappropriate use of data collected for one purpose—in this case, to provide for passports—for another purpose. In that case, the misuse was political—one assumes that somebody was curious or wanted to see if President Obama might really been born in Kenya or something like that.

But the story that nobody hears of is that we have the tools now—the audit tools—to uncover the wrongdoing. The contractors who hacked the file were discovered within days, punished, fired, and lost their jobs. That's exactly appropriate.

Now, if you take our current state in the intelligence community that I've been talking about and put it in this context, the parallel argument would be that we shouldn't collect data for passports because someone could misuse them. And that would be, self-evidently, the wrong answer. In the Department of State, we have the right paradigm. We collect the data, we put it to appropriate uses that are good government uses, and then when people misuse the data, we punish them. We audit to find out who has done wrong and we make sure that they can't do it again.

The right answer today, in the intelligence space, is the same one. Instead of doing what we've done for the last seven years, which is to deny ourselves this type of analytical capacity in the intelligence community because of our fears of abuse, we should revise our thinking, reinvigorate that sort of research, develop the tools that will lead us forward and allow us to do the analysis that give us a better chance of catching somebody like Abdulmutallab.

If we don't do that, if we don't change how we treat this veritable flood of intelligence data, the one thing we can be sure of is that the Christmas plot will happen again. And we'll be sitting here talking to ourselves four days from now, or four years from now, asking the same questions we are asking today, about how something like that could happen.

And the answer will also be the same: We will have done it to ourselves. ▪

# Rising China's Fate

## GORDON G. CHANG

A review of
*Rising China and Its Postmodern Fate* by Charles Horner
2009 University of Georgia Press

---

R ising China and Its Post-modern Fate is a sweeping intellectual history of the last three impe-rial dynasties—the Yuan, Ming, and Qing—and the subsequent Republican and communist peri-ods, a span of more than seven hundred years. Why do we care about Chinese history?

We care because, as author Charles Horner notes, China's past has an extraordinary influence on its future. Even though present-day

Chinese historians reject Mao Zedong's instruction to "use the past to serve the present"—in other words, to distort history for current political purposes—they are nonetheless busy creating an imagined narrative, one that "can inform a new generation's grand designs."

As Horner, a Hudson Insti-tute scholar writes, "China is seek-ing to assemble a set of lessons from the country's past that can serve as a guide, and even an inspi-ration, for China's return to promi-nence and power in the world." It's no wonder the country's intellec-

Gordon G. Chang is a Forbes.com columnist and the author of *The Coming Collapse of China*.

tual scene is now among the most vibrant anywhere, bringing together ideas from all points of the globe, mixing them, and somehow making the brew "Chinese."

And what are China's citizens now thinking? To control the popular narrative, the central government has imposed its interpretations of history, some of which are obviously ahistorical, on the population. Yet the effort to formulate its own truth is creating difficult-to-resolve dilemmas for Beijing, and that is a particularly acute problem because the Communist Party constantly seeks to legitimize its more recent policies "by finding relevant antecedents in past heroic epochs." And there is no more heroic epoch than the Qing dynasty, the last one.

Horner notes that in 2002 the State Council, the central government's cabinet, employed 400 scholars to complete a history of Qing rule by 2012, the centennial of the abdication of the dynasty's last emperor. Just how dangerous a task this is became evident in 2003. Then, China Central Television, the state broadcaster, was airing a 59-part Qing-era epic entitled *Toward the Republic.*

About half way through the television series China's censors took out their scissors due to perceived problems with the storyline. For one thing, the episodes were garnering high ratings as viewers began to think that, due to the Westernization efforts of late-Qing rulers, the dynasty might have evolved into a democracy, thereby avoiding the bloodshed of Sun Yat-sen's revolution. Not to mention Mao's. Beijing's censorship then turned into a debacle as uncut versions of the episodes began circulating throughout the country. The current regime's problems caused by the television series means that the subtitle of Horner's book— *Memories of Empire in a New Global Context*—seems particularly apt.

As the author astutely notes, the Party's Qing problems are not over yet. When the official history comes out in two years, "attentive Chinese" will realize that "the modern Chinese state is more a Qing product than has previously been admitted." For China's authoritarian leaders, already obsessed about their right to rule, no idea could be more subversive than the notion that the Communist Party has not in fact transformed the Chinese state, as Mao and his successors so loudly promised to do.

So we should not be surprised that Horner writes that "the specter of the collapse of communism" haunts China's current leaders. Their rule may, from the outside, seem secure, but they sit atop a country increasingly difficult to control. "Though 'China' is often thought of as something fixed and immutable," he writes, "it has shown instead that it can change its shape, organize itself in different ways, relate to the world in different ways, and alter the ways it thinks about the world." After all, this book charts the transformation of the country as "Confucian China" became "Modern China," which in turn made itself into "Rising China." And the process continues as "Rising China" looks to the future when it will inevitably change into "something else."

And what will that be? As Horner points out, the Chinese supremos face a crucial decision. As their nation continues to rise, they could retain the current international system and have China supplant the United States at the head of it. Or they could try to change the system altogether so that it is more to their liking.

Horner hints it will be the latter. After all, Beijing's political system is not well suited to the world as it now is. "China's basic mode of governance—'democratic centralism,' an increasingly creaky arrangement based on a now universally repudiated Leninist political theory—runs contrary to a worldwide trend, if not toward classic representative democracy then at least toward greater decentralization," he notes toward the end of his superb work. Or to put this thought more succinctly, postmodernism is haunting China. So to secure their rule, Chinese leaders need to fundamentally change the world around them.

Yet that bold attempt will undoubtedly be filled with danger for them and their nation. China is currently thriving because its economy is well suited to servicing postmodern societies, and the country has therefore prospered in the peace and stability guaranteed by the United States. The Communist Party's attempts to change that American-led international system are sure to create *luan*—chaos—on a global scale. So in their attempt to win the world, communist leaders could end up losing their own nation. That just may be, to use Horner's well-chosen words, China's "postmodern fate." ∎

# Time Bomb

## PAULA DeSUTTER

A review of
*The Rise of Nuclear Iran: How Tehran Defies the West*
by Dore Gold
2009 Regnery Publishing

S uccessive U.S. Administrations have sought to change through diplomatic engagement the behavior of the Iranian regime since the 1979 Islamic Revolution. Engagement has taken indirect and direct form. The Europeans have also tried diplomatic engagement, culminating in high level engagement from 2003 through 2008 on the nuclear issue. All such efforts have

Paula DeSutter served as Assistant Secretary of State – Bureau of Verification, Compliance and Implementation from 2002-2009. Ms. DeSutter is the author of *Denial and Jeopardy: Deterring Iranian Use of NBC Weapons.*

failed. Indeed, they may have created an even more dangerous situation by demonstrating fecklessness and weakness that Iran may further exploit, to the detriment of efforts towards deterrence.

Enter President Barak Obama. Promising a new approach, the Obama Administration has advocated yet more engagement. Obama's engagement, however, offers an "unclenched fist" and direct talks, and eschews preconditions such as halting enrichment of uranium. As charming and persuasive as Mr. Obama may be, thus far his offers have been rejected by the Islamic Republic. But President Obama has also said that this approach could not be carried out indefinitely.

Dore Gold's *The Rise of Nuclear Iran: How Tehran Defies the West*, offers a well-researched and well argued tutorial on the history of the West's efforts at engagement, the reasons for their consistent failure, and the urgency of finding a better set of tools. The failure of the West to respond effectively to Iran's support for terrorism, to Iran's participation in the murder of Americans directly in Iraq and through Hizbollah and al-Qaida in Lebanon and Saudi Arabia, and to Iran's pursuit of nuclear weapons in violation of its obligations, has led Iran, reasonably, to conclude that the West is weak and thus it can pursue these programs with impunity. Having failed to deter Iran thus far, Gold underscores the risk that we will be unable to deter Iran from even more threatening behavior.

Gold demonstrates that Iran has consistently used these Western efforts at engagement to solidify and expand the very actions the West has sought to stop via negotiations.

As a result, Iran has laid the ground-work for a global terror network and for the development and delivery of nuclear weapons. Gold explains how Iran has used Taqiya, or dissimulation and deception, perhaps best exemplified

by a 2006 speech by Iranian Ambassador Hassan Rowhani, in which he explained that his engagement with the West had bought time for advancement of Iran's uranium enrichment program, to defeat Western efforts at deterrence and dissuasion.

Gold's discussion of Taqiya with regard to hostage taking, Afghanistan and Iraq is excellent. However, Gold seems to believe that Iran's use of arms control and negotiations for cover and concealment of pursuit of weapons of mass destruction began in 2002 after the existence of their covert nuclear program became public.

I believe Iran's tactics started a decade earlier, and that its decision to pursue nuclear, chemical and biological weapons was made earlier still. While it is probably true that Khomeni originally declared that weapons of mass destruction were non-Islamic, by the mid-to-late 1980s, the position changed. As I reported in *Denial and Jeopardy: Deterring Iranian Use of NBC Weapons*, by 1987 and 1988, Rafsanjani was publicly articulating the need for them, noting that "Although the use of such weapons is inhuman, the war taught us that international laws are only scraps of paper."

Numerous statements and announcements by the regime articulated pursuit of WMD and training, including offensive tactics for chemical and biological weapons use. Following Desert Storm, Iran realized that open pursuit of WMD was dangerous. Their public statements then reversed to advocacy of arms control.

Gold also does a very good job of articulating the challenges to deterring the current Iranian regime given Ahmadinejad's belief in the immanent coming of the Hidden Imam or Mahdi. There is, however, a point Gold does not address: In Shiism, while defensive jihad may be declared in defense of the faithful, only the Hidden Imam can declare an *offensive* jihad. Therefore, Ahmadinejad's conclusion that the Hidden Imam has returned, or that he can receive communication from him, would enable a pre-emptive attack.

What then does Gold recommend to strengthen deterrence? In addition to highlighting the need for Western realism in any diplomatic engagement with Iran, he proposes two steps: first, adoption and implementation of the Kyl-Bayh "Iran Refined Petroleum Sanctions Act." He also, however, argues that "If the West has a choice between negotiating yet again with the regime in Tehran or undercutting it further, it should clearly promote a process that leads to its collapse and replacement." Here, one wishes there were more.

Encouraging the people of Iran without giving some measure of real support is likely only to lead to their deaths. Covert action is unlikely to be any more productive now than in the past.

Is there nothing further that can be done? Gold points out much earlier in the book, for example, that following the July 1998 downing of IranAir 655 by the USS Vincennes, Iranian provocations in the Gulf appeared to be deterred. Are there lessons from that accidental assertive action that can be replicated?

How can efforts to undermine the economy be turned against the regime and not their unwilling and unhappy population? Moreover, how can these policies be implemented rapidly enough to stop the Islamic Republic's rapid march towards a nuclear weapon?

Gold skillfully articulates the threat, how it has evolved, how it has been aided and enabled by the lack of a robust and meaningful response by the West to punish the murderers of American soldiers and Marines and to deny Iran the benefit of their actions. Let us hope that Gold's cautionary tale of how Iran uses engagement to further its deadly policies will be read and understood in the White House and in Foggy Bottom. ▪

# Strong Horses

## ROBERT R. REILLY

A review of
*The Strong Horse: Power, Politics and the Clash
of Arab Civilizations* by Lee Smith
2009 Doubleday Books

L ee Smith's *The Strong Horse* is a book of personal discovery. It is both entertaining and full of that kind of wisdom that only real experience brings after it has been thought over and fully digested by a critical mind.

Much of what Smith says about the true nature of the problems in the Middle East is available elsewhere, and in greater depth, from scholars and other journalists in the field, like Bernard Lewis and David Pryce-Jones. The merit of this work is in seeing how a young man without many preconceptions waded into the Middle East, mastered its language, and experienced its culture. It is an enticing, engaging memoir. Smith did not emerge empty-handed from his eight-year sojourn to Cairo, Beirut and Jerusalem.

However, many of Smith's admonitions and lessons-learned may be difficult for Washington policy makers to embrace because he has

Robert R. Reilly is a former director of the Voice of America and a board member of the Middle East Media Research Institute. His forthcoming book is *The Closing of the Muslim Mind* (ISI Books).

come to the conclusion that many of the problems in the Middle East are intractable, and therefore not amenable to policy solutions. This is never welcome news in Washington, where policy solutions is a business.

But even a broader perspective is necessary to appreciate why what Lee says may not be compatible with a number of schools of foreign-policy thinking on the Middle East, on either side of the aisle. For many years, Great Britain and France did the heavy lifting in the Middle East until, exhausted after World War II, they withdrew or were driven out, usually with the encouragement of US anti-colonial policy. We thought, in fact, that the problems in the Middle East were the result of British and French occupation (and of Ottoman occupation before that). Remove the colonizers, and the Arab peoples would naturally assume the blessings of self-government and liberty. With this in mind, we pressured the British and French to withdraw from their mandates. They did. During this period, the United States was very popular in the Middle East.

Now, however, the United States had to shoulder the responsibilities of keeping order and, needless to say, an open supply of the increasingly important oil supply. Thus, without even realizing it, we inherited the mess resulting from the dissolution of the Ottoman Empire. The United States

soon learned that the problems of the Middle East were not all of colonial origin; they were indigenous. This is when the United States began to become unpopular. While some of these problems seemed to have been subsumed during the US-Soviet rivalry, they are back today with a vengeance in Iraq, Lebanon, Syria, Gaza, Iran and elsewhere.

How was the US supposed to think about and deal with these issues? When years of experience demonstrated the impenetrability of Islam's adherents to Christian evangelization, Americans simply secularized salvation to forms of education, health care, and economic development necessary for democracy, the spread of which would achieve the earthly redemption of the Middle East. This is still largely our policy, or at least the thinking behind it, as carried out by the State Department and USAID.

President George W. Bush reverted to a pre-WW II perspective that simply substituted homegrown Arab tyrants for the role of the colonial oppressors. If the Arab tyrants were removed, the Arab people would naturally assume self-government. On this basis, but for other sound reasons as well, we went into Iraq.

The problem, of course, is that the culture of the Middle East is not naturally amenable to the democracy policy solution. The great value of this book is to show the many ways in which this is so. The book is all the more compelling because these were not Smith's views when he arrived. There is even a scene before his departure, when he visits and thanks Edward Said, of all people, for arousing his interest in the Middle East. Experience was his teacher.

The book is called *The Strong Horse* because of Smith's realization that the primacy of power that rules in the Arab world is essential to its culture. He locates some of its source in Arab tribalism (on this subject, the classic work is *The Closed Circle* by David Pryce-Jones). It is fascinating to read his accounts of how well-intentioned American efforts to bring democracy are interpreted by its potential beneficiaries:

> The assumption that democracy was all a plan to set the Arabs at each other's throats also made sense to many Arabs because it fit with the way they see their own societies.

"The way they see their own societies" is something we need to understand before we go writing any more policy prescriptions for the Middle East. Smith's book is both a warning and a big help in this respect. He also is clear that those in the West who are calling for an Islamic Reformation as a solution to the problems there do so unaware of the fact that the Islamism *is* the Islamic Reformation; it has already happened. That is why we, and many Muslims, are in so much trouble.

There is one element missing from Smith's analysis of the "political pathologies" he encountered, and that is their origin in Islamic spiritual pathologies. The "strong horse principle" is ultimately rooted not in Arab tribalism but in a strong horse idea of God that elevates the teaching that "right is the rule of the stronger" to a theological level. Finally, it is a deformed theology that has produced the dysfunctional culture of the Middle East. But that is the next place to look, once one has understood all that Smith has so ably offered here. ▪

# Worlds of Islam

## CHRISTINE BRIM

A review of
*The World of Islam*
2010 Mason Crest Publishers

W ho would have thought that a middle-school book series on Islam, often meticulously balanced volumes, each a mere 64 picture-filled pages, could prove controversial? Yet the "World of Islam" series did exactly that when its publication was announced in February 2010. The reason? The series presents a mostly complete and surprisingly detailed factual presentation of Islam in history and in the present day. That fact-based historical account is sadly lacking in most school textbooks, according to Gilbert Sewall, former education editor for *Newsweek*, founder of the American Textbook Council and editor of the study "Islam in the Classroom: What the Textbooks Tell Us."

Sewall's 2008 whitepaper shows the persistence of non-factual—but oh-so "multicultural"—representations of Islam in textbooks for all grades, K-12. Check your child's history textbook and you'll see what he is talk-

Christine Brim is the Chief Operating Officer of the Center for Security Policy.

ing about. As Sewall notes: "One stratum of US thought—one that is influential in school publishing today—resists ugly facts about Islam that involve violations of liberal ideals and dangers to international security. To worry about Islamic revivalism or to object to a controlling Islamic 'voice' in the nation's history textbooks, no matter the reason or argument, violates multicultural convention and is thus politically risky. Epithets such as 'Islamophobia' deaden the debate."

Thus, the need for a balancing series of books to supplement that "c o n t r o l l i n g    I s l a m i c 'voice'," achieved two years after Sewall's landmark study with these ten books—of varying quality individually, but as a package, a well-done and serious addition to school libraries and classrooms. In the curriculum-politics debate, "The World of Islam" is a historic effort to replace the politically correct disinformation prevalent in so many current textbooks with that novelty, actual documented historical fact. One is tempted to send the series to MSNBC, CNN and the increasingly Saudi-owned FOX News, along with the many supporters of "engagement" with the Muslim world in the White House, the Pentagon, the State Department.... so many readers, so little time.

We will take up a collection for that worthy cause at the end of the review. But first, the controversial recent history of this series.

The World of Islam is a ten-volume series of books for middle school and high school students published in February 2010 by Mason Crest Publishers, an educational publisher in Broomall, Pennsylvania. The Foreign Policy Re s e a r c h    I n s t i t u t e ' s (FPRI) Wachman Center, which seeks to promote civic and international literacy in the classroom, served as editorial consultant on the project. FPRI is a venerable institution, founded in 1955, one of the earliest post-WWII think tanks.

One does find a range in quality of analysis and sheer scholarship among ten books, written by authors varying from world-class experts in their discipline, to freelance authors with no other listed credits. Yet the act of reading any of these books is akin to watching a tightrope act. The authors proceed precariously but with élan, telling hard truths in a determinedly calm tone. The editorial meetings must have gone long into the night, and would make a fascinating publication in themselves.

Each book is a serious effort, usually successful, to give the student enough knowledge about Islam to develop his own perspective in spite of the "multicultural" narrative of most textbooks and many teachers. Conveniently, each book has an overview introductory chapter on Islam, so if a student reads only one of the set of ten books, he'll still have some general knowledge.

Which brings us to the question of why so well-meaning and frankly innocuous a series of history books for middle-schoolers might upset those ultra-sensitive vigilantes against "Islamophobia," that unindicted terrorism finance co-conspirator, the Council on American-Islamic Relations (CAIR). On March 17, CAIR-PA in Philadelphia held a press conference "to announce the launch of a nationwide campaign to challenge anti-Islam bias in a series of children's books that the Washington-based Muslim civil rights group says promote 'hostility toward Islam and suspicion of Muslims'." The next day The Philadelphia Inquirer quoted Moein Khawaja, "civil rights director of CAIR-PA, complaining that passages in the books were "inflammatory."

Daniel Pipes, director of the Middle East Forum headquartered in Philadelphia and a former director of the Foreign Policy Research Institute wrote that same day, quoting from internal CAIR emails about the book series, in which Khawaja had said "I've been given the entire order list for this series (orders that came in up until yesterday). This list shows which school districts and libraries have purchased the individual books or entire series—it is a nationwide campaign. This is valuable infor-

mation because we can contact each of them and explain that they really got propaganda. I'm not sure what legal issues there are here - but there has to be some sort of thing about masked propaganda in schools and libraries?"

Even more revealing is another of these CAIR emails, also quoted by Pipes. Karen Dabdoub of CAIR's Cincinnati chapter replied that she shared Khawaja's concerns: "Many of these authors have names that at the very least sound Jewish and none that sound like Muslim names. While I know we can't judge a book by its cover it still gives me reason to doubt the balance of the information in these books."

In spite of their best efforts to ban the "World of Islam" series as "masked propaganda," CAIR-PA's campaign against the books appears to have had beneficial, if unintended consequences, drawing attention to the series and encouraging parents and community groups to purchase them for their school and local libraries.

Since I would recommend exactly that - purchasing the whole package for your local libraries - here is a summary of the individual books in the series. All of these books are good enough, some better than others, and the series as a whole is significantly more accurate than regular textbooks.

**DOROTHY KAVANAUGH:**

**The Muslim World: An Overview**

This first volume is by Dorothy Kavanaugh, a freelance writer whose books include *Islam, Christianity, and Judaism* (2004), *Islam in Africa* (2006) and *Islamic Festivals and Celebrations* (2010). Here's an accurate but politically incorrect passage, quite representative, discussing the origins of the Quran: "Yet the words of the Qur'an were not written down during the lifetime of Muhammad, who could neither read nor write.... Over the years, some messages were written down on pieces of bone or scraps of paper. Others were passed down orally... as a result, there were many variant texts, though these have been suppressed and Muslims deny they ever existed."

And equally accurate—on political "Islamism" such as the Muslim Brotherhood movement:

> Islamism is a sociopolitical movement that seeks to implement Shariah law wherever Muslims live. Islamist movements around the world are engaging in an ideological struggle against Western civilization and values. The most extremist groups promote jihad through the use of terrorism. Much of the time, Islamist ideology also contains an anti-Semitic strain.

Not the stuff of your usual CAIR interview on TV, and quite heartening to think honest statements could breach the classroom walls this way.

**BARRY RUBIN:**

**The History of Islam**

The second volume is by Dr. Barry Rubin, director of the global Research in International Affairs Center of the Interdisciplinary University, and editor of the Middle East Review of International Affairs Journal. Dr. Rubin is widely respected, and pulls no punches:

> While Muhammad is always seen in Islam as a mortal being, he is also held up as the ideal model of a man and of proper behavior. This creates certain problems given his marriage to a nine-year-old girl and his involvement in warfare, torture and assassination of his enemies.... Another problem is that actions legitimized by Muhammad, the Qur'an, and the Sunna (the traditions of early Islam)—which are seen as being ordained by God—cannot be abrogated by later human decisions. Thus, wife-beating (albeit limited in extent), amputation for thefts, and a death sentence for apostasy from Islam can be ignored by governments or even Muslims but cannot formally be changed in terms that are seen as officially revising Islamic beliefs and practices.

Arguably hard to comprehend for the White House, but manageable for a 10th grade World History student. In a scant 64 pages he covers the Sunni-Shia Rift, the Abbasid Dynasty, the Ottoman, Safavid and Mughal Empires, and Islam in the

Modern World, including modernism from 19th Century reformers to the Islamists, the Muslim Brotherhood, the Iranian Revolution and al-Qaeda. He ends on a chipper note, stating that "Islamism" is not likely to triumph, as it is not supported by most Muslims.

### DOROTHY KAVANAUGH:
### Islamic Festivals and Celebrations

This third volume in the series is again by Dorothy Kavanaugh. The author presents a conventional overview on Islamic festivals, though it is quite lacking on Ramadan. Ramadan is a theo-political celebration which celebrates both the Muslim belief that this is the month of Mohammad's first revelation and—left out in the book—the month of the genocidal battle of Badr against the Quraysh tribe. Ramadan is both a spiritual and military holiday, emblematic of that duality which pervades Islam. You would never know that from this volume which presents a happy and superficial view of Islam.

### JOHN CALVERT:
### Divisions Within Islam

The fourth book in the set is by John Calvert, the Fr. Henry W. Casper Associate Professor of History at Creighton University, where he teaches courses on me-

dieval and modern Islamic history. A workmanlike discussion of Sunni Islam, Karijites, Twelver Shiism (and the Hidden Imam), the Ismailis, other Shia subgroups, and Sufism.

### ABE M. COHEN:
### The Monotheistic Religions: Judaism, Christianity, Islam

The fifth book is by Abe M. Cohen, who is a freelance writer with no other listed credits. It is a dispensable volume, unfortunately—well-intentioned perhaps, but finding far too much parity and moral equivalency among the three faiths to be accurate. The volume does manage to point out that the Islamic reinterpretations of the Old Testament are far different than the originals. But quite the least good of the lot of ten books.

### TANYA SKLAR:
### Islamic-Jewish Relations Before 1947

The sixth volume is written by Tanya Sklar, a research assistant at the Global Research in International Affairs Center. Sklar's work is an even-handed survey, discussing the limited and conditional tolerance of the so-called "golden age" of Islam, but also the long history of Islamic Anti-Semitism chronicled extensively by Andrew Bostom in his book on the same topic. It includes the historical account of the massacre of the Jewish Qurayza tribe in 628, when 700-

900 tribesmen were beheaded in Medina and women and children sold into slavery or kept as slaves by Mohammed and his men. For those students who have been taught that the founding of the state of Israel is the origin of all Islamic Jew-hatred, this will be an eye-opener.

Indeed the "Period of Conquest" chapter treats this period for what it was, a military conquest of surrounding areas, and includes a detailed discussion of dhimmitude and paying the jizya tax. One of the better volumes in the series.

### MICHAEL RADU:
#### Islam in Europe

Michael Radu is Co-Chair of the Foreign Policy Research Institute's Center on Terrorism, Counter-terrorism and Homeland Security, and author or editor of books including *Europe's Ghost: Islamism and Jihad in Western Europe* and *Dilemmas of Democracy and Dictatorship: Place, Time and Ideology*, and others. Just the fact that this volume is included is encouraging; that students have a chance to learn about one of the most important geopolitical trends that will affect them, without a rose-colored filter (or more properly, without the red-green filter of the Left/ Islamist bias that usually prevents discussion, much less serious study, of these topics).

Radu properly emphasizes the problems of unlimited immigration and increasingly radicalized Muslim populations. However, he leans towards an inaccurate moral equivalency between Islamists on the one hand, and those who would protect their national cultures and political institutions from Shariah on the other:

> One has to be wary of the claims of both sides in the European Islam debate. Many Muslim organizations claim that any criticism of any Muslim practice—whether polygamy, honor killings, or forced marriages... constitutes Islamophobia (hatred of Islam) or racism. On the other hand, growing populism and nationalism in some European countries (especially Denmark, the Netherlands, and Austria) tends to falsely associate all immigrants with Muslims and Islam, and all Muslims with terrorism and practices unacceptable or illegal in Europe....

A poorly constructed comparison (Muslim organizations on the one hand, versus concepts such as "populism and nationalism" on the other), that we can hope will be repaired in future editions. And when Radu is good he is really good, as in this observation:

> Nevertheless, many among the British establishment reason that these groups are not part of al-Qaeda, which is true; that they are growing in power, which is regrettably true as well; and that they are composed of reasonable men with whom Britain can do business, which is patently untrue.

Now wouldn't you like to have that sitting on a desk in No. 10 Downing Street?

### ANNA MELMAN:
#### Islam, Law and Human Rights

This eighth book in the set is by Anna Melman, Deputy Editor at the Global Research in International Affairs Center and the Assistant Editor of *Turkish Studies Journal*. Brilliantly, Melman starts her volume on Shariah with a discussion about human rights as understood in the West—and only then defines Shariah Law and what human rights are reduced to under that totalitarian and barbarous system. This is where the series shines, and this one book should be required reading for Congress, state legislatures and American judges who now face the possibility of Shariah law being used in US courts as it is in UK courts. She points out that, historically, Muslim majority countries have varied in how much power they gave to Shariah law versus secular law; but with the ascendance of the Muslim Brotherhood and related Islamist political parties, Shariah's power is increasing, and as a demonstration she cites a 2008 report that 66% of Egyptians, 60% of Pakistanis and 54% of Jordanians favor Shariah as the only source of legislation. Our allies, in short, who are rapidly regressing away from whatever real or fantasized modernism we projected onto them in the last century.

### ANNA MELMAN:
#### Islam in America

Anna Melman is also the author of this volume, a good overview positively packed with statistics and cases, showing the changing trends in Muslim immigration here in the US. From Estevanico, a slave born in Morocco who arrived in Florida in 1528, to the South Asians and Iranians who fled civil wars and revolutions in the 1970s and 80s, to current times when "some Muslims in the United States also began to support Islamist ideology and the transformation of American society into a Muslim nation." She does point out, to the book's credit, the disastrous results of current immigration policy within the Muslim community itself: earlier generations—most of whom came to America to escape Shariah law—now face current immigrants, many of whom have come to America to impose it.

"These second-generation Americans may sympathize with a pan-Islamist, and sometimes militant, revivalist ideology," she writes. She relies, as do all the authors, on Pew polls perhaps too exclusively, but for many issues Pew is the only organization surveying the American Muslim community. Yet she also makes the crucial distinction that the majority of Muslim Americans, unlike Muslim

Europeans, do not feel marginalized—presumably because of the great economic, business and social success Arabic and South Asian Muslims have achieved on average in the US, in general making more money and getting more advanced degrees than the statistical (and always dolefully underachieving) "average American."

Unfortunately, students will learn little about the status of women in the Muslim American community here. And the tone of careful neutrality can be strained:

> In many places in the United States, the growth of the Muslim population has caused public agencies to be sensitive and adapt to their religious needs or claimed requirements...in response, these institutions have faced criticism for accommodating Muslims at the taxpayers' expense and blurring the line separating religion and state.

That's walking a fine line successfully, although "claimed requirements" is the key to addressing the imposition of Shariah. The section on Muslim Organizations is adequate, given the limits of the book. She describes ISNA, for example, as a group that "aims to promote an ideological approach that sees Islam as a total system of life, not a religion confined to the mosque..." And she discusses the Jamaat-i-Islami links of ICNA and the Muslim Brotherhood links of the Muslim American Society. She takes CAIR's description as "the largest Muslim civil rights and advocacy group" at face value, but at least she notes that they have been accused of harassing or slandering critics of radical Islamism. And she notes that these groups have a primary goal which is to change America policy towards Israel.

Best of all, the book includes a detailed presentation on Islamic Charity Organizations, including the multi-million dollar budgets, the Saudi connections and the litany of groups from Holy land Foundation to Global Relief to the al Haramain Islamic Foundation. The book does need to be updated, since it states that the Holy Land Foundation trial ended in a hung jury in October 2007, when of course the retrial resulted in convictions for all accused. A revised edition updating all these current events will be welcome.

## ALAN LUXENBERG:
### Radical Islam

The final volume in the World of Islam set is by Alan Luxenberg, Vice-President of the Foreign Policy Research Institute, also author of *The Palestine Mandate and the Creation of Israel*, part of another FPRI series for middle and high school students from a ten-volume series on "The Making of the Modern Middle East." A solid and sober discussion of the topic, the history and breadth of the major radical organizations and individuals.

Let's hope these ten books mark a beginning trend in countering the disinformation in children's textbooks imposed by the far left and Islamist advocacy groups.

Mason Crest Publishers and FPRI have shown that facts still matter, that history is not a tissue to be rewoven with each political fad, and that CAIR's book-banning "campaign" was a feeble and short-lived attempt at bullying. Consider purchasing a set for your local school or public library, or just mail one to 1600 Pennsylvania Avenue—and light a candle in a dark time. ▪